BEYOND BUDGETING

7 Modern Challenges to Saving Money

Chris Garrido

Copyright © 2024 Chris Garrido

All rights reserved

No part of this book may be reproduced, or stored in a retrieval system, or transmitted in any form or by any means, electronic, mechanical, photocopying, recording, or otherwise, without express written permission of the publisher.

This material is intended for general public use. By providing this content, Park Avenue Securities LLC and your financial representative are not undertaking to provide investment advice or make a recommendation for a specific individual or situation, or to otherwise act in a fiduciary capacity. Guardian, its subsidiaries, agents, and employees do not provide tax, legal, or accounting advice. Consult your tax, legal, or accounting professional regarding your individual situation. Chris is a Registered Representative and Financial Advisor of Park Avenue Securities LLC (PAS). OSJ: 4200 W Cypress St., Suite 700, Tampa FL, 33607, 813-289-3632. Securities products and advisory services offered through PAS, member FINRA, SIPC. Financial Representative of The Guardian Life Insurance Company of America® (Guardian), New York, NY. PAS is a wholly owned subsidiary of Guardian. Westshore Financial Group Inc is not an affiliate or subsidiary of PAS or Guardian. 6995665.1. This material has not been endorsed by Guardian, its subsidiaries, agents, ot employees. No representation or warranty, either express or implied, is provided in relation to the accuracy, completeness, or reliability of the information contained herein. In addition, the content does not necessarily represent the opinions of Guardian, its subsidiaries, agents, or employees.
ISBN-13: 9798340137166

Printed in the United States of America

CONTENTS

Title Page

Copyright

Introduction — 5

Chapter 1 — The Struggle to Save: — 9
Exploring the Psychology of Money

Chapter 2 — Internal Spending Pressures: — 17
Our Natural Tendencies to Spend

Chapter 3 — External Spending Pressures: — 27
Spending Cues from the Outside World

Chapter 4 — The Credit Card Trap: — 33
How Debt Can Derail Savings

Chapter 5 - The Stock Market Mirage: — 41
Alluring Returns Can Lead to Overspending

Chapter 6 - The Cost of Living Surge: — 49
Understanding Inflation's True Impact

Chapter 7 - The Savings Priority Shift: — 57
Why Traditional Budgeting Misses the Mark

Conclusion — 69

About The Author — 73

INTRODUCTION

Each year, millions of people face retirement with empty wallets and shattered dreams, despite their best intentions. Maybe they lived beyond their means or waited too long to start saving money. Maybe they were unprepared for an unexpected emergency. Maybe they were never taught how to effectively plan and save money for the future. Or worst of all, maybe they got bad financial advice.

Traditional financial planning often revolves around maximizing returns from investments, but this approach has failed many people. Focusing solely on returns can overlook the underlying emotions, behaviors and habits that affect financial health.

Fortunately, there is a new generation of financial planning that has shifted its focus from just selling stocks and bonds to a more holistic approach centered around personal behaviors. This method involves a deep dive into understanding *why* individuals struggle to save enough money. It addresses key factors such as spending habits, financial goals, and emotional triggers related to money.

In today's world, saving money can be tough due to rising costs, job market uncertainties, and increasing reliance on credit. Traditional budgeting methods often fall short in this environment. But there's hope. By adopting new strategies and changing how we think about financial health, we can overcome these challenges and find financial stability.

In this book, we'll dive into modern strategies and practical steps to help you navigate today's financial world. We'll cover how to manage your cash flow, handle debt, boost your savings, and make smart choices with your money. You'll learn how to build financial habits that fit seamlessly into your lifestyle, rather than forcing you to conform to outdated practices. Saving money is like building muscle; it requires consistent exercise and training to see lasting results. But like ***physical*** fitness, ***financial*** fitness goals often go unmet in the absence of education, planning and emotional buy in. This book will guide you in strengthening your "savings muscle," making the accumulation of wealth a more natural and effortless part of your life.

We'll tackle common pitfalls and offer practical solutions tailored to today's realities. This guide will help you create financial practices that work for your family and set you on a clear path to long-term financial success. Together, we'll turn financial challenges into opportunities for a more secure and prosperous future. Let's start this journey to take control of your financial health and transform obstacles into stepping stones.

CHAPTER 1:
THE STRUGGLE TO SAVE

Exploring the Psychology of Money

Saving money isn't just a matter of math; it's also a mental challenge. There are psychological hurdles that make it difficult, and these often stem from how we think about saving money in relation to our values and emotions. To understand why this can be so hard, we need to look at the difference between **adaptive values** and **core values**.

Adaptive Values vs. Core Values

Adaptive values are traits that help us tackle immediate challenges and meet short-term goals but tend to fade over time. Adaptive values include things like discipline, hard work, and self-control. While these traits are important for saving money, they often involve discomfort and can feel unpleasant. For example, saving money means we must resist the urge to spend and make sacrifices, which can be tough and not very enjoyable. **Core values**, on the other hand, are the deeply held beliefs that define what is most meaningful to us. These might be values like family, security, freedom, or happiness. When our actions align with our core values, we feel more motivated and connected to our goals and are more likely to find long-term success.

The Problem with Saving Money

Saving money has historically been linked to adaptive values like discipline and hard work. This means that the act of saving can feel like a constant struggle, much like a restrictive diet. Just as diets that are too strict can be hard to stick with, saving money by cutting back on spending can feel like a hassle. The immediate discomfort of what we are denying ourselves can overshadow the long-term benefits, making it easy to give up. For example, think about dieting. Many diets require cutting out our favorite foods or sticking to strict eating rules, which can feel like a punishment. As a result, people might start with enthusiasm but soon find it hard to keep up, leading to frustration and failure. Similarly, saving money often involves the discipline of sticking to a strict budget that doesn't allow for fun things like going to the movies and coffee at Starbucks. That can feel restrictive, and the immediate discomfort can make it hard to stay committed.

How to Make Saving Money Feel Better

To overcome these challenges, we need to connect saving money to our core values. Instead of focusing on the discipline and hard work required, we should retrain our brains to focus on how saving money helps us achieve what matters most to us. For instance, if family security is important to us, we can view saving money as a way to provide a stable future for our loved ones. If freedom is a core value, saving money might be seen as a path to financial independence and the ability to make choices that truly matter. If education is a core value, saving money might be the way we ensure our kids go to college. And if family is a core value, saving money could be the way to take that trip of a lifetime together. Which is better – a vacation to Florida this year or a vacation to Italy in 3 years? The difference between these two trips lies in successfully saving money. By linking the act of saving money to the core values that mean the most to you, the process becomes more meaningful and less about making sacrifices.

My Personal Experience: *"In more than a decade of working as a financial advisor, I've helped hundreds of families save and grow their money for future goals. Over time, I've improved my approach, but the biggest change* *came when I shifted from focusing on the discipline of financial wellness to instead talking about the possibilities. Hard work alone doesn't connect with our values, hopes, and dreams. No one works hard just for the sake of working hard; we work hard to achieve something meaningful. Hard work and discipline are tools we use to reach our goals, not the goals themselves.*

The issue is that we tend to avoid hard work when it doesn't align with what's truly important to us. When I first meet a client, I ask about their future goals. If they say they want to buy a boat, I dig deeper: "What kind of boat? What size? What color? What will you name it? Who will you bring aboard? How will you feel on the water with the wind in your hair?" Their answers create an emotional blueprint of their future. Hard work and discipline are like the hammer and nails that will help build that plan into reality, but the alignment with their core values is what will ensure the project continues to completion.

*But in finance, we often make the mistake of focusing too much on the tools rather than the dream. I encourage you to keep in mind **why** you're working hard, and I believe you'll find more success. Hard work for its own sake can feel pointless; it needs to be tied to something meaningful.*

I teach my son the value of hard work every day. When he works hard toward his dreams and core values, I feel immense pride. However, if he spent his Saturday digging a tunnel from our front yard to the neighbors' house, I'd likely be frustrated and tell him to fill it in. You could argue that he worked hard on that tunnel, but for what? The problem is that too many people are focused on hard work, but working hard is wasted and hard to maintain if it's not connected to something that really matters.

Here's an exercise: Before you start a plan to save money, sit down and identify your core values. What is most important to you? What has always been important to you? Why is it important to you? How could obtaining the things that matter most improve your life? What could it feel like when you accomplish these goals? How can increasing savings help you achieve your future dreams? How much of your income can you commit to saving each month to support your core values and turn your dreams into reality? This is a radical departure from budgeting, discipline, hard work and other adaptive values that often lead to frustration and giving up. Framing your mindset to focus on the things that matter most to you will likely lead to more positive outcomes."

Practical Tips for Aligning Savings with Core Values

1. **Identify What Matters:** Take some time to think about what's really important to you. Is it family, security, freedom, or something else? Understanding your core values helps make your savings goals more personal and relevant.
2. **Set Meaningful Goals**: Create savings goals that reflect those core values that you've identified. For example, if family security is a core value, you might set a goal to build an emergency fund or save to become a homeowner.
3. **Find Enjoyable Ways to Save:** Look for saving methods that you find satisfying and that align with your values. For instance, if you find value in experiences, you might save for a special family vacation. If you like to compete, consider setting up a savings competition and incorporate family members.
4. **Visualize the Benefits:** Regularly remind yourself of how saving money connects to your core values and the positive outcomes it will bring. Visualization can keep you motivated and make the process feel

more rewarding. Perhaps make a Vision Board. (Don't laugh!)
5. **Celebrate Progress:** Acknowledge and celebrate your achievements along the way. Recognizing your progress reinforces the connection between your saving efforts and your core values, making the journey more enjoyable.

Conclusion

Saving money can be challenging because it often feels like a struggle tied to discipline and hard work, which are adaptive values. However, when we connect saving money to our core values—what matters most to us—we can make the process more meaningful and motivating. By focusing on how saving money helps us achieve our long-term goals and aligns with our core values, we're more likely to overcome psychological barriers and be successful in our efforts to save more.

CHAPTER 2: INTERNAL SPENDING PRESSURES

Our Natural Tendencies to Spend

In today's world, we're used to getting what we want right away. Whether it's a new gadget, takeout food, or a spontaneous trip, we're constantly surrounded by ways to satisfy our desires instantly. But while these quick fixes might feel good now, they often come at a price: our financial health and future savings.

The Drawback of Instant Gratification

Instant gratification is the desire to experience pleasure or fulfillment without delay. We live in a world where things move faster than ever. The result is that we can practically have whatever we want whenever we want. However, when we chase instant gratification, we hurt our ability to save money because we're always tempted to buy things ***right now*** instead of waiting.

Our parents' generation knew how to handle this better; they planned and saved up for big purchases, often using layaway plans to avoid debt. Many of you reading this book may not even remember layaway. (Google it.) By contrast, when we need something immediately, we tend to buy it whether we have the available cash or not. Often that results in us using credit cards - spending money we don't actually have. This not only makes those items more expensive due to interest charges but also keeps us in a cycle of debt and financial stress. (More on credit cards later.)

This desire to have everything right away can make it harder to save for important goals like buying a house, paying for education, or preparing for retirement. Instead of focusing on long-term plans, we get caught up in short-term pleasures, leaving us unprepared for financial emergencies, opportunities and other future expenses. If we took a step back and followed the example set by previous generations, we could better manage our finances and save money more effectively. It's like the Nestle Quick bunny taught us as children – "Patience is a virtue."

The Cost of Convenience

Not only do we want everything right now, but we also want it to be easy. Online shopping, especially on platforms like Amazon, has made spending money easier than ever before.

With so many options available and the convenience of buying from the comfort of home, it's simple to buy things on a whim. However, that ease of access can lead to impulsive buying. This is compounded by the fact that these online retailers often have our credit card data stored. We don't even need to go into the other room and get our credit card out of our purses or wallets anymore. We can truly purchase anything, often with a simple click of a button. The one-click purchasing option removes the natural friction that occurs when making a purchase in person. Without the physical act of handing over cash or swiping a card, the psychological barrier to spending is lowered, making it easier to overspend or purchase items that weren't originally planned. We don't ask ourselves, "Do I really need this?" or "Can I really afford this?" nearly as often when purchasing through an online platform.

The Challenge of "Lifestyle Creep"

Lifestyle creep, or lifestyle inflation, is what happens when our spending goes up every time we get a pay raise or a financial boost. Instead of saving that extra money, we often use it to improve our standard of living. This might mean buying a fancier car, moving to a bigger house, eating out more, or splurging on luxury items. What starts as a small change can quickly lead to bigger, ongoing expenses. For instance, if we use a raise to buy a new car, it might seem like a good idea. But then we end up spending more on insurance, maintenance, and gas. Over time, these additional costs can eat up the benefits of the raise, leaving us no further ahead financially.

Example: John makes $100,000 per year. Each year he gets a 4% raise. (Some of you may be thinking, "I don't get a 4% raise each year, so this doesn't apply to me." Even if you don't get scheduled steps up in pay annually, it is still very likely that you'll make more money 20 years from now than you do today, in the same way that you likely earn more today than you did 20 years ago.)

Over the course of 20 years, the total of just his annual raises equals nearly $1 million. If he continues to live off the $100,000 each year and commits to saving the 4% pay raises, he has $977,700 saved up. And that's not factoring in the potential growth of investing those savings each year. However, if he ups his lifestyle by 4% each year, there is nothing left at the end of 20 years, and he has squandered the opportunity to save nearly $1 million.

If any of you are so inclined, here's the math:

$$\text{Total Salary} = 100{,}000 \times \frac{(1 + 0.04)^{20} - 1}{0.04}$$

$$\text{Total Salary} = 100{,}000 \times \frac{(2.191123 - 1)}{0.04}$$

$$\text{Total Salary} = 100{,}000 \times 29.777$$

$$\text{Total Salary} = 2{,}977{,}700$$

$$\text{Total Raises} = 2{,}977{,}700 - 100{,}000 \times 20$$

$$\text{Total Raises} = 2{,}977{,}700 - 2{,}000{,}000$$

$$\text{Total Raises} = 977{,}700$$

I know what you're thinking, "Inflation!" And you're right. Everything in John's world got more expensive over those 20 years, so the idea that he could comfortably live off $100,000/year 20 years later is naïve. But like most things in life, there is a balance. Let's say that John increased his lifestyle by 2% each year and committed to saving the additional 2%. At the end of 20 years, he would have saved more than $400,000. If he invested the money annually and averaged a 6% Rate of return, he would have accumulated more than $700,000 over 20 years. There is incredible *savings potential when our income goes up. The magic lies within controlling how much you keep.*

My Personal Experience: *"In my experiences with clients I have found that all of us have money leaking out of our lives each month due to our natural urge to spend. Generations ago, life was harder, and people were natural savers. Today life has gotten easier, and our natural tendency is to spend money. Too often in my industry, people overcomplicate the idea of finance. I like to oversimplify it. Money can only do two things – it either gets saved or it gets spent. That's it! We either keep it or we give it away. At its core, personal finance really is that simple, and saving money is about identifying and eliminating as many of the variables in our life that push us to spend money rather than save it.*

These urges are very real. In fact, my wife would tell you that no one dislikes waiting for purchases more than I do. I met her 16 years ago when she worked at a clothing store, and I kept coming back to buy more shirts. I didn't really need the extra clothes; I just needed time to convince her to go out with me. Talk about impulse buying! During those months, if the shirt I wanted was out of stock, she would suggest ordering it online and having it shipped in 5-7 days. But every time, I'd choose a shirt I liked a bit less so I could take it home right away. I'm extremely prone to instant gratification. I'm the same way with online shopping. I only look at items on Amazon if they're available with 'Prime' shipping. I find it funny that now waiting more than two days for a purchase to arrive feels unacceptable. Still, there are ways to practice patience and save money more effectively, even for people like me."

How to Manage Our Natural Impulses to Spend

1. **Wait Before You Buy**: Before making a non-essential purchase, wait at least 24 hours. This "Cooling Off Period" can help you decide if you really need the item or if the urge will pass.
2. **Stick to a Shopping List**: Write down what you actually need before shopping online and stick to that list. This helps prevent impulse buys.
3. **Turn Off One-Click Ordering**: Disable one-click buying features on online stores. Adding a step to the purchasing process can give you time to think twice about the purchase.
4. **Plan Ahead for Major Purchases**: Set aside funds over time to ensure you're financially prepared before making nonessential purchases. Stick to your

savings plan and avoid impulsive spending to make sure you can afford the item without straining your finances.

5. **Build an Emergency Fund**: Prior to making a large purchase, save up money for any potential unexpected expenses. Having this safety net means you're less likely to rely on credit for emergencies or opportunities after making your purchase.

6. **Compare Prices**: Check prices on different platforms and consider shopping at physical stores to make sure you're getting the best deal and really need the product.

7. **Control Lifestyle Creep**: When you get a raise at work, set aside a specific percentage for savings before making any purchases.

Conclusion

Each of us has a natural urge to spend money. These urges like instant gratification and convenience come at a cost and make it tougher to save money for the future. So can using pay raises to fund unnecessary lifestyle upgrades. By understanding how these habits affect our spending and adopting better financial practices, we can take control of our natural urge to spend money. It's important to balance immediate desires with long-term goals to achieve financial stability and success. With a bit of awareness and planning, we can make smarter choices and be better prepared for what lies ahead.

CHAPTER 3: EXTERNAL SPENDING PRESSURES

Spending Cues from the Outside World

Unnecessary spending to fulfill our desire for instant gratification is an internal pressure on our finances. The desire to spend comes from *within* each of us. However, there are also *outside* triggers all around us that we may not even realize are causing us to spend more money. From the eerily specific ads we receive each day, to the pressures we sometimes feel watching our friends' lives play out on social media, these external influences can make it significantly harder to maintain a healthy savings plan. Understanding and navigating these pressures is important for achieving financial wellness and reaching long-term goals.

The Power of Targeted Marketing

One of the most common external pressures we face each day is a constant stream of targeted ads and marketing. Companies use advanced technology to show us ads that seem to know exactly what we want. It's almost like our phones and computers are eavesdropping on us. For example, you might talk about wanting a new gadget, and then you see ads for that gadget popping up everywhere.

These personalized ads are designed to make you feel like you need to buy right now. When you see something that seems perfect for you, it's hard not to give in and make a purchase. This convenience and constant flood of tailored suggestions make it easy to spend more than planned, which can hurt your savings.

The pressure of these ads is compounded by the ease of online shopping. We discussed in the previous chapter that with just a few clicks, we can go from browsing to buying. This convenience reduces the time we might otherwise use to reconsider whether a purchase is truly necessary. However, you're also likely to be prompted to buy other suggested items while you shop online. These suggestions are often based on your previous purchases, so they feel very customized to your preferences. This constant stream of personalized suggestions can make it challenging to resist the urge to spend, thus derailing our savings goals.

The Pressure to Keep Up with the Social Media

Another significant external pressure comes from social comparisons. The saying "keeping up with the Joneses" captures the constant desire to match or surpass the lifestyle of those around us. Whether it's new gadgets, stylish clothing, or luxurious vacations, there's a relentless push to keep pace with family, friends, or even social media influencers.

Social media makes this worse by showing us the highlights of other people's lives. Seeing friends' new cars or vacations can make us feel like we need to spend money to fit in or show off. This comparison can lead to unnecessary spending as we try to match the lifestyles of others, even when it means exceeding our spending or going into debt.

This comparison isn't just about having cool stuff; it's also about feeling good about ourselves. We might end up buying things we can't afford just to keep up an image. This cycle of trying to keep pace with others can lead to spending money we don't have and possibly hurting our savings goals.

Social media influencers can make it harder for us to save money as well. By constantly showing off the latest products, fashion, and experiences, they create a glamorous image of their lives that makes it seem like we need to buy these things to be happy. By promoting expensive items and making them look essential, influencers make us feel like we're missing out if we don't spend. How many of you ran out to buy a Stanley cup earlier this year? That 100-year-old company had a rebirth in 2024, largely on the backs of social media influence. No longer was Stanley the brand for rugged campers. Now they make must-have, daily essentials for soccer moms. This pressure to keep up with trends and fit in with their lifestyle can lead us to spend more impulsively, often at the expense of saving. The more we see these idealized images, the harder it becomes to resist buying things we don't really need, making it tough to stick to a savings plan.

My Personal Experience: *"I spend most of my days helping clients to maximize the efficiency of their cash flow. When I started in this industry, the nonessential spending I saw was typically limited to coffees at Starbucks or splurging on an $8 Netflix subscription. Today, I work with families who have $500/month in Amazon purchases, and they typically can't recall much of what they bought. How many times have you arrived home to an Amazon package at the door and had no idea what was in the box? The pressures of targeted marketing, social media and peer influence have us spending money like never before. When I was younger, a mentor explained to me the difference between sales and marketing to me. He said, "Chris, everyone likes to buy things, but no one likes being sold to. Marketing gives people the **opportunity** to buy. When you try to **make** them buy, that's Sales." That concept stuck with me, and it's more relevant now than ever.*

Recently, I saw an Amazon ad with a tiny image I couldn't make out. I clicked to zoom in, and it turned out to be a ping pong table. Over the next several days, I got 17 ads for ping pong tables from social media, Amazon, and email marketing. I wasn't actually looking to buy a ping pong table; I just couldn't see the image. But if I had been in the market for a ping pong table, I'd have been faced with 17 more opportunities to buy it. I would have had to exhibit restraint and say no 17 more times. That's a lot to ask. It's no wonder people make impulse purchases and struggle to build their nest egg. My mentor was right on the money. Today, we're bombarded with endless "opportunities" to spend. Marketing is more targeted and persistent than ever, making it harder to resist unnecessary purchases and save money for the future. But there are steps you can take to help."

Navigating These Pressures

To effectively manage the external pressures that make saving money harder, consider the following strategies:

1. **Limit Exposure to Targeted Ads**: Be mindful of your online activity and adjust privacy settings to limit the amount of data companies can collect about you. Use ad blockers or opt-out of targeted advertising when possible.
2. **Disable Notifications**: Turn off notifications for shopping apps and social media platforms to avoid being constantly reminded of sales and promotions.
3. **Limit Social Media Use**: Reduce the time you spend on social media platforms where you're likely to encounter influencers, peer spending and ads. Set specific times for social media use and stick to them.
4. **Unfollow Influencers**: If certain social media influencers or accounts frequently promote products you find tempting, consider unfollowing or muting them to decrease their influence on your spending decisions.

5. **Be Critical of Marketing**: Develop a habit of questioning whether you really need an item or if it's being marketed to you in a way that manipulates your emotions or desires.
6. **Focus on Personal Values**: Shift your attention from comparing yourself to others to focusing on what genuinely matters to you (core values). Invest in experiences and items that align with those values rather than what's trending.

Conclusion

External pressures such as targeted marketing and the need to keep up with others can make saving money feel like an uphill battle. By recognizing these influences and taking proactive steps to manage them, you can better align your spending habits with your long-term financial goals and core values. Remember, achieving financial stability requires both awareness of these pressures and a strategy to avoid them. With mindful strategies and a clear focus on your personal financial goals, you can navigate these challenges and build a more secure financial future.

CHAPTER 4: THE CREDIT CARD TRAP

How Debt Can Derail Savings

Let's face it—credit cards can be a serious roadblock to our savings goals. We often think of them as a convenient way to manage our finances, but they have a way of sneaking into our lives and creating serious problems. Let's dive into how credit cards can quietly derail our efforts to save money and build wealth.

The Hidden Costs of Spending Money We Don't Have

One of the biggest issues with credit cards is that they make it too easy to spend money we don't actually have. We swipe our cards, thinking we're only borrowing temporarily, but the reality is that this habit can turn into a long-term financial problem. Each time we use a credit card, we're effectively putting ourselves in debt. The more we use it, the harder it becomes to pay off that debt, especially when high interest rates come into play.

Interest Rate Drag

Speaking of interest rates, let's not forget how they can turn a small amount of debt into a huge financial burden. Credit cards often come with sky-high interest rates. For example, if we have $15,000 in credit card debt at a 25% interest rate, the costs quickly spiral out of control. Over a 20-year period, if we only make minimum payments, we could end up paying around $52,000 in interest alone—more than three times the original debt. That's $52,000 that could have gone towards our savings, investments, or other financial goals. This is what we call "lost wealth" - money that could have been growing for us but instead is wasted on interest payments.

Delayed Recognition of Spending

Another sneaky issue with credit cards is that they delay our recognition of spending. When we make a purchase, we don't see the bill right away. It typically takes weeks for that bill to show up. By the time we receive it, we've probably spent even more money, and the total debt keeps piling up. This delay makes it easy to lose track of how much we're really spending and how quickly our debt is growing.

The Illusion of Rewards

And then there's the temptation of credit card points and rewards. They seem enticing, don't they? Every time we spend, we earn points or cashback, which feels like we're getting something for free. But here's the catch: these rewards are designed to encourage us to spend more. We're essentially being rewarded for spending money we don't have, creating a dangerous feedback loop that silently becomes a habit. Every time we use our credit card to earn points, we're reinforcing the habit of spending beyond our means. This habit becomes ingrained, making it even harder to save money.

The Debt Cycle

Credit card debt can trap us in a vicious cycle. The more we use our credit cards, the more of our future cash flow gets diverted to paying off debt. This reduces the money we have available to save, invest, or spend on things that truly matter. For many, this means living paycheck to paycheck, struggling to make ends meet, and feeling stressed about finances, and the problem is more alarming than ever before. As of 2024, credit card debt in the United States has reached historically high levels. Here are some key statistics and insights into the current state of credit card debt:

1. **Total Credit Card Debt**: According to the Federal Reserve Bank of New York, the total outstanding credit card debt in the U.S. surpassed $1 trillion in early 2024. This marks a significant increase from previous years and reflects the growing reliance on credit cards for both everyday expenses and larger purchases.
2. **Average Credit Card Debt Per Household**: The average credit card debt per U.S. household is approximately $6,500. This average debt can vary widely depending on the household's income, spending habits, and financial situation. (*source: Experian*)
3. **Credit Card Debt Trends**: Credit card debt has been rising steadily, with a notable acceleration in recent years. For example, in the past year alone, credit card debt increased by over $80 billion, driven by higher consumer spending and the effects of inflation. (source: *American Bankers Association*)
4. **Interest Rates**: The average annual percentage rate (APR) for credit cards has also risen, now averaging around 19% to 20%. This high interest rate

contributes significantly to the overall cost of carrying a credit card balance.

5. **Demographic Insights**: Certain demographics, including younger adults and low-to-moderate income households, are disproportionately affected by high credit card debt. These groups often face greater challenges in managing and repaying debt due to limited financial resources and higher debt-to-income ratios.

These statistics highlight the significant burden of credit card debt on American households and underscore the importance of financial management and debt reduction strategies.

My Personal Experience: *"One of the most overlooked ways that credit cards can hinder our ability to successfully save money is the psychological affect. Many of my clients have felt a shift in focus away from wealth building and toward immediate debt relief. The stress and anxiety of managing credit card debt can lead to poor financial decisions, such as reducing contributions to savings or investments. Worse yet, I have seen families cash out their 401(k) and pay taxes and early withdrawal fees to eliminate credit card debt.*

Too many people that I meet think of savings and debt elimination as an "either-or" proposition. The fact is that the two are not mutually exclusive. I believe that more people should save to eliminate debt. Instead of focusing solely on overpaying credit card bills to rapidly eliminate the debt, consider putting that energy into aggressive saving. By doing so, you can build up a substantial amount of money that allows you to pay off the debt in large chunks. Rushing to eliminate debt without saving first can lead to more debt when unexpected expenses arise. If all your money goes to paying off MasterCard, you'll have nothing left to handle surprises, forcing you to use your credit cards again and restart the cycle. On the other hand, saving to pay off credit card debt also helps you get used to the habit of saving. This way, once the debt is cleared, you're less likely to fall back into the trap of accumulating new credit card debt."

Breaking Free

To break free from this cycle, we need to face the truth about how credit cards can undermine our financial health. Here's what we can do:

1. **Limit Credit Card Use**: Try to use cash or debit cards for purchases. This way, we're spending the money we actually have.
2. **Pay Off Balances**: Aim to pay off credit card balances in full each month to avoid interest charges.
3. **Create a Budget**: Stick to a budget that helps us manage our spending and avoid accumulating credit card debt.
4. **Build an Emergency Fund**: Having a financial cushion can reduce the need to rely on credit cards for unexpected expenses.
5. **Educate Ourselves**: Understand the true cost of credit card debt and the impact of interest rates on our finances.

Conclusion

While credit cards offer convenience and rewards, their impact on our ability to save money can be profound and detrimental. The high interest rates, coupled with the temptation to spend beyond our means, often lead to a cycle of debt that erodes our nest egg over time. Additionally, the delayed recognition of spending and the allure of points and miles can further cloud financial judgment, making it easy to overlook the true cost of credit card use. By recognizing the ways credit cards can work against our financial goals, we can take steps to limit their impact and shift our focus to building real wealth. It's time to take control and make choices that support our long-term financial health.

CHAPTER 5: THE STOCK MARKET MIRAGE

Alluring Returns Can Lead to Overspending

Most people consider high stock market returns to be a good thing when it comes to saving money for retirement, and they're right. But sometimes the allure of high stock market returns can actually work against your savings goals. Relying too heavily on the idea of big returns might jeopardize your ability to build your savings effectively. By understanding the risks and limitations of stock market investments, we can better prepare ourselves to manage our investments wisely and ensure our savings efforts are on track for a secure future.

Rate of Savings vs. Rate of Return

Let's get real about something that's all too common - the illusion that chasing high returns in the stock market will make up for a lack of savings. We see the headlines about stock market booms, and it's easy to get hooked on the idea that a big return will solve our financial problems. But here's the hard truth: rate of return doesn't matter nearly as much as rate of savings.

Let's break this down with an example. Imagine two people: Alex and Jamie. Alex decides to save 20% of her income but doesn't invest it, while Jamie saves just 5% of his income but gets a hefty 10% annual return on his investments. Which one do you think will accumulate more wealth?

Fast forward 30 years. Alex has consistently saved 20% of her income. Jamie, on the other hand, has only saved 5% of his income but has enjoyed a 10% return on his investments. Guess what? Alex ends up with more money. Yes, you read that right. Even with Jamie's high returns, Alex's disciplined saving yields a bigger nest egg over time. Why? Because saving more consistently has a compounding effect that typically outstrips the gains from higher returns. The math doesn't lie: saving more consistently trumps the gains from chasing higher returns with fewer contributions.

Here's the catch: people often think a higher expected rate of return gives them permission to save less money. They start spending more on immediate pleasures, thinking they'll make it up later with their investments. This is a classic mistake. It's not just that they're spending more; they're also taking a dangerous gamble with their future.

Emotional Responses to Down Markets

Here's another potential pitfall. Let's say Jamie's high returns came with higher risk. When the market takes a downturn—and it will—Jamie might panic. We've seen it time and again - investors see their portfolio lose value, and their first reaction is to pull out of the market entirely. They want to stop the bleeding, but in doing so, they miss out on the typically inevitable rebound. This knee-jerk reaction often leads to missing out on long-term gains and permanently undermining financial futures.

Consider this hypothetical: Jamie invested in high-risk stocks, and during a market dip, his portfolio value plummeted. Overwhelmed by the loss, Jamie pulls his money out, avoiding further drops but also missing the subsequent recovery. Meanwhile, Alex, who stuck to her savings plan and avoided risky investments, sees her money grow steadily over time. Jamie's impatience and reactionary moves mean he misses the long-term wealth creation that Alex benefits from.

The Effects of Taxes and Fees

Many people don't think about taxes and fees when looking at potential investment returns. Historical rates of return are usually shown before these costs are taken out, so the actual returns are often lower. For investments in regular (non-qualified) accounts, you pay capital gains taxes on the profits you make when you sell them, which can reduce your overall gains. These taxes can take a bite out of your earnings. In retirement accounts like 401(k)s or IRAs, you don't pay taxes until you withdraw the money, but then those withdrawals are taxed as regular income. Plus, investment fees, like management fees or fund expenses, can also eat into your returns. So, even though high return rates look great, the real returns you get after taxes and fees are usually lower. This is why it's important to factor in these costs when planning your investment and savings strategies.

My Personal Experience: *"The impact of stock market returns on the amount of money people save is something I see often, and it's alarming. It's also a bit counter intuitive. You might think that higher market returns would make investors want to put **more** money into the market, but in my experience the opposite is often true. It's as though the allure of great market returns gives them the permission slip to* *save less money and spend more. The truth is that it's our rate of savings that drives future wealth, more so than our rate of return.*

When I first meet with clients, I often find that their primary savings are limited to their 401(k) or 403(b) accounts, typically with contributions of less than 6% of their income. Surprisingly, many believe that these modest contributions will be sufficient to ensure a comfortable retirement. However, market returns are neither guaranteed nor predictable. Even with favorable returns, insufficient contributions will likely lead to insufficient retirement income. Additionally, most retirement calculators assume ideal investor behavior, including consistent returns and remaining invested through market downturns. Given that many clients struggle to remain committed during significant market declines, managing their emotions is as crucial as managing their investments. Ensuring that their investment strategies align with their risk tolerance is a key part of my job."

Steps to Build Lasting Wealth

So, what's the lesson here? It's straightforward: systematize and maintain a high savings rate. This means saving a significant portion of your income consistently, regardless of what the stock market is doing, and creating a system where your savings contributions are being made automatically. Use your savings to build an emergency fund that can handle the unexpected. Then, invest wisely to work towards your long-term financial goals.

1. **Commit to a Savings Rate**: Determine a realistic savings rate and stick to it. Aim for at least 15-20% of your income. The key is consistency. Automate your savings so you don't have to think about it each month. The same way you set up automated bill pay through your bank, you can set up a regular automated savings draft.
2. **Build an Emergency Fund**: Save enough to cover 3-6 months of living expenses in a readily accessible account. This fund will help you weather unexpected events without derailing your financial plans, in spite of stock market conditions.
3. **Invest Wisely**: Once your emergency fund is in place, start investing wisely. Rather than chasing rate of return and going "all in" on the hottest stock tip, try to diversify your investments to manage risk. Focus on long-term goals rather than chasing high returns.

4. **Avoid Emotional Decisions**: Stay the course with your investments, even during market downturns. Panic selling can lock in losses and prevent you from benefiting from market recoveries. Stick to your investment strategy and rebalance your portfolio periodically.
5. **Educate Yourself**: Continuously learn about personal finance and investing. Understanding the fundamentals will help you make informed decisions and avoid being swayed by flashy, high-return promises.
6. **Regularly Review and Adjust**: Periodically assess your savings and investment plans. Adjust your strategy as needed based on changes in your financial situation, goals, or market conditions.
7. **Seek Professional Advice**: If you're unsure about your investment strategy or financial plan, consider consulting a financial advisor. They can provide personalized advice based on your specific goals and risk tolerance.

Conclusion

Don't get swayed by the allure of high returns. Instead, focus on saving a substantial portion of your income. This is the real game-changer. The key to building lasting wealth isn't about chasing flashy returns; it's about maintaining the discipline to save regularly and the wisdom to invest wisely. By committing to a high savings rate, creating a solid financial foundation, and staying the course through market ups and downs, we position ourselves to benefit from long-term growth. In the end, it's our consistent efforts and prudent financial management that truly drive wealth creation, not the pursuit of risky, high-return investments.

*All investments contain risk and may lose value. Diversification does not guarantee profit or protect against market loss.

CHAPTER 6: THE COST OF LIVING SURGE

Understanding Inflation's True Impact

Inflation isn't just about the obvious price hikes we see at the grocery store or gas station. It's a sneaky force that slips into every corner of our financial lives, silently munching away at our savings in ways we might not always notice. Sure, inflation makes everything more expensive, and it's easy to see how that affects our savings. But inflation also hides in less obvious places, disrupting our finances in ways that can be hard to pin down. Let's dig into how inflation affects us beyond the obvious and explore some hidden costs that might test our ability to save money more than we realize.

The Hidden Cost of New Technology

Twenty years ago, we didn't have smartphones. The idea of nearly everyone carrying a tiny computer in their pocket was still science fiction. Fast forward to today, and smartphones are everywhere, but they don't come cheap. An iPhone or its equivalent can set us back hundreds (if not thousands) of dollars every few years, and that's not counting the cost of data plans and accessories. Then there's the flat-screen

TV—something that's now standard in nearly every home. Twenty years ago, these things didn't exist, but now we're spending more money on bigger screens with fancier features.

What will the next 20 years bring? Maybe personal robot butlers or other advanced technology that we can't even imagine yet. The point is that each new technology often comes with a hefty price tag and a cycle of frequent upgrades. These costs can add up quickly and erode our nest egg.

Planned Obsolescence: A Seldom Talked About Expense

Another sneaky way inflation gets us is through planned obsolescence. Many products are designed to wear out or become outdated, prompting us to replace them more frequently than we might expect. Think about tires, roofs, and washing machines. These are essential items with finite lifespans. A roof that lasts 20 years or tires that need replacing every few years add up to significant costs over time. The longer we own these items, the more likely we are to face replacement costs. This continuous cycle of spending on replacements can gradually drain our savings account balances.

The Rising Costs of Healthcare

As we get older, healthcare becomes a bigger part of our lives and budgets. Healthcare costs have been skyrocketing for decades. For instance, the average annual premium for employer-sponsored family health coverage has more than doubled over the past 20 years. In 2004, it was about $10,500, and in 2024, it's over $23,000.[1]

Elder care costs are even more staggering. The average cost for a private room in a nursing home is now about $108,000 per year. With these costs rising faster than inflation, it's clear that healthcare is a significant and growing expense that can seriously affect our ability to save money if we're not prepared.

The Soaring Price of College Tuition

College tuition is another area where inflation has hit hard. Twenty years ago, the average annual cost of in-state tuition and fees at a public university was around $4,000. Today, it's over $10,000.[2] Private colleges have seen even steeper increases. These rising costs mean more student loans and higher financial strain for families. If we're saving money for our children's education, we need to account for these climbing expenses and adjust our saving strategies accordingly.

Overspending and Inflation: A Dangerous Mix

When inflation drives up the cost of living, it's easy to overlook personal overspending. We might justify that new gadget or extra dining out as just a side effect of rising prices. But this mindset can mask the real issue: our spending habits. It becomes harder to track where our money is going when it feels like we're constantly pouring cash into a leaky bucket. Inflation can make it seem like our expenses are justified when, in reality, they might be masking habits that are compromising our financial well-being.

My Personal Experience: *"One of the things I'm most proud of in my financial planning practice is how we focus on cash flow. We put a lot of effort into teaching clients how money moves in and out of their lives and how they can save more by adjusting their spending priorities, (which I'll explain more in the final chapter). Managing cash flow starts with knowing what your monthly expenses are. These costs vary by family, but there's a clear trend: most families I work with are spending 50% to 100% more now than they did 8 to 10 years ago. For example, families who used to* *spend $8,000 a month are now spending $12,000, and those who spent $10,000 are now spending $15,000. Living costs keep going up, and while people often blame price tags, the real issue is more complex.*

We rarely think about the impact of things like healthcare on our rising costs of living. As we age, our healthcare needs usually increase, and healthcare costs often rise even faster than regular inflation. I recently saw this firsthand with a client. At 55, he had a severe stroke and needed months of hospital and rehab care. After 60 days of care, his insurance company notified the family that his benefits had run out. They were given the option to continue his care out of pocket at a cost of $60,000 a month!!! Never in a million years would my client have believed that he would require round-the-clock care at such a young age. And never in a trillion years could he have imagined how expensive it would be. This cautionary tale illustrates the importance of sound financial principles. Life isn't getting cheaper, which means we must get better prepared."

Steps to Protect Against Hidden Inflation

To help safeguard our savings from the inflation squeeze, here are some practical steps we can take:

1. **Save Money Systematically:** Set aside a percentage of our income before we even see it. Treat savings like a non-negotiable expense, not a leftover. Automate this process by setting up direct transfers to savings or investment accounts. Prioritizing saving money over lifestyle expenses ensures we consistently build wealth, regardless of how inflation might affect our day-to-day finances.
2. **Track Spending Closely:** Keep a close eye on our spending and compare it to previous years. This helps us identify whether higher costs are due to inflation or if we're spending more than we should.
3. **Plan for Healthcare Costs:** Include potential healthcare costs in our long-term financial plans. Consider investing in health savings accounts or other vehicles that can help us manage these expenses tax efficiently.
4. **Prepare Early for Education Costs:** Start saving early for college and consider education savings accounts that can grow over time.

5. **Invest Wisely:** Diversify investments to include assets that historically keep pace with or outpace inflation.
6. **Manage Technology Upgrades:** Be mindful of the costs associated with new technologies. Consider whether an upgrade is necessary and explore budget-friendly options.

Conclusion

Inflation impacts more than just the cost of everyday items like eggs and bread. As we grow older, the expenses associated with our lives increase in numerous and often unexpected ways. By recognizing and preparing for these hidden costs of inflation, we can more effectively save money and plan for the future, keeping our financial goals within reach. Although inflation is a persistent challenge, with thoughtful planning and proactive strategies, we can mitigate its effects and safeguard our financial futures.

---

[1] *"Employer Health Benefits Survey," Kaiser Family Foundation 2004 and 2024*

[2] *"Trends In College Pricing," CollegeBoard 2023*

CHAPTER 7: THE SAVINGS PRIORITY SHIFT

Why Traditional Budgeting Misses the Mark

Traditionally, managing cash flow meant using a budget. Here's the problem; budgets typically don't work. Budgeting requires meticulously planning and tracking every dollar we earn and spend. This method focuses on balancing "what comes in" against "what goes out." While this approach may have worked for some in the past, more times we hear about families that have struggled to "stick to a budget" and ultimately failed. Budgeting is time-consuming and stressful, but that's not even the biggest failure. The biggest problem with budgets is that they plan to spend and do not plan to save.

Think of a to-do list with ten tasks. You're much more likely to complete tasks 1 and 2 than you are tasks 9 and 10. Similarly, when we budget, we decide how to spend our money first at the top of the list, and then try to save whatever's left, (if there's anything left at all), at the bottom. Just like the last few items on a to-do list often get overlooked, the money left over after budgeting for expenses is usually minimal, leading to insufficient savings. What we prioritize gets done. If we make spending money the priority, saving money will always fall short.

Luckily, we now have a better way to handle our money: prioritizing our cash flow correctly. When we manage the order in which we spend and save, it makes our financial lives simpler, and we don't have to track every penny. By focusing on the right cash flow priorities, we can avoid the hassle of detailed accounting and make sure our financial choices support both our current needs and future goals. But what exactly does it mean to prioritize cash flow properly?

The Order of Cash Flow

We all have various aspects of our lives that involve financial costs, such as protection, savings, debt, taxes, and lifestyle expenses. Prioritizing these areas and deciding which to address first can help us manage our finances more effectively and potentially save more money. This proper cash flow prioritization is the secret to ensuring that the most urgent areas are addressed first, and that unnecessary spending does not interfere with our ability to save money.

Protection First and Fully

Protection should be our primary financial focus because ensuring that we have sufficient life insurance, disability insurance, and liability protection for our home and car insurance is critical to securing our future income. Most of us are millionaires in waiting. The millions of dollars that we stand to earn throughout our career represents our most asset, and unforeseen events such as illness, lawsuits, or premature death could wipe it out at any moment. Therefore, safeguarding our income and assets with proper insurance protection must be our most urgent financial priority. Hence, the first dollars we spend should be to protect our future income (the most valuable asset we own).

Save Before You Spend

Once your assets and future income are fully protected, the next step in efficiently managing cash flow is deciding how much money to save. It might seem odd, but it's important to set aside a percentage of your income for savings *before* paying your bills. Most people pay bills first and then save what's left, which typically means that saving money takes a backseat to spending. As a result, we often find ways to spend whatever is left, leaving nothing left to save. Simply focusing on cutting expenses (budgeting) isn't enough because it still prioritizes spending over saving money. It's like saying, "I value spending money more than saving it, but I'll cut back on my Netflix subscription each month to save money for retirement." These minor sacrifices that we are willing to make when we budget pale in comparison to what is possible when we commit to saving money before we spend it. This is not just a change in the way we spend money, it's a monumental shift in the way that we think about our finances. This approach starts with committing to save a fixed percentage of our income first—say, 20%—and then managing our lifestyle with the remaining 80%. This bumps saving money up to the top of the to-do list. Prioritizing savings in this manner ensures that funding our long-term financial goals comes before immediate desires, leading to greater financial security and a more fulfilling future.

Life Events Fund

Once the commitment to saving money has been made, the next decision is where those contributions should go. Retirement accounts like 401(k) and IRAs are helpful in building long-term savings, but what about short-term needs? Those accounts tend to feel "illiquid" or hard to access, given that withdrawals can incur taxes and fees. One common mistake we make is neglecting to build and maintain a Life Events fund. Often called an emergency fund, this financial reserve should not only cover unexpected emergencies but also provide funds for potential opportunities that may arise. Many times, we will prioritize spending money or even eliminating debt without having built up a Life Events fund. This short-sighted approach can lead to financial challenges, especially when life presents us with unexpected events. Or worse yet, we don't have sufficient money saved, and that lack of liquidity (accessible money) forces us to start up the debt cycle again. Yes, sometimes aggressively trying to eliminate debt without a Life Events fund can lead to more debt. Cash acts as the shock absorbers for life, allowing us to adapt to unforeseen opportunities or events. Building a sufficient Life Events fund – as a rule of thumb I suggest 6-12 months' income – can prevent life's curve balls from derailing our financial goals.

Debt vs. Savings

Another common mistake is prioritizing debt repayment over saving money. We often focus on eliminating low-interest debt while neglecting other crucial financial needs.

For instance, paying off a car loan with a 3.5% interest rate might seem wise, but if we're not also contributing to our retirement account or Life Events fund, we risk compromising our long-term financial stability. The same principle applies to aggressively paying down a low-interest mortgage. Not all debt is equal, and managing it wisely is only one aspect of our overall financial health. It's important to understand that saving money and paying off debt are not mutually exclusive. We should work on both simultaneously, but not before ensuring our finances are protected against unexpected events.

Lifestyle vs. Savings

Lifestyle expenses should be the last priority in cash flow management. While this may sound harsh, it can actually be quite liberating. Once you've ensured that your finances are protected, have funds available for unexpected events, and have allocated the necessary savings, you can freely spend the remainder as you wish. This is a significant departure from cutting out small luxuries like lattes or canceling subscriptions, which can feel restrictive. Instead, this approach ensures that protection and savings are handled first, allowing you to use the rest of your money however you like.

Prioritization is crucial. Focusing on lifestyle expenses before addressing savings may offer immediate gratification but can jeopardize long-term financial stability. Spending more on dining out, travel, and entertainment can enhance short-term enjoyment, but neglecting savings can hinder your ability to build an emergency fund, plan for retirement, or invest in future goals. Balancing today's pleasures with a "save before spending" mentality helps create a more sustainable and enjoyable lifestyle both now and in the future.

My Personal Experience: *"When I present my idea of ideal cash flow prioritization to clients, it's usually met with confusion. Admittedly it is an uncommon approach, but it is deeply rooted in common sense. Consider a work sponsored retirement account like a 401(k). Those contributions represent a commitment to saving a percentage of our income before it ever gets a chance to get spent. Furthermore, the contributions are automated, removing the need for human discipline. Imagine if it was up to us to mail a check in to our 401(k) company every pay day. How much less money would we all have in our accounts? How many times would we forget, or worse yet, find something to spend that money on instead? We will never know! That's the secret. Because that money is being saved before we ever* *have a chance to think about spending it, we have no clue what we would have purchased with those dollars. Our 401(k) creates a "forced automatic savings" in our lives. We never see that money. It never hits our bank account. We never get a chance to spend it. It always gets saved - Every time!*

Humans are highly adaptable creatures, for better or worse. We will make different spending decisions based on the amount of money that's available to be spent. At its worst, that means that when we make more money, we are likely to spend more money. But at its best, that means that when there is less money available to be spent, we will spend less. I sometimes use the example of a high electric bill. One time I got one that was over $800, and I almost had a heart attack. But I still paid the bill. It was nearly $400 more than I was expecting, but I still paid it because I had no choice. So, what did I not buy that month that I would have purchased if I'd kept that extra $400? I have no idea, and I never will know. Because I never had the chance to spend it, what I would have purchased never even crossed my mind. I just gave the electric company $400 extra and lived off what was left.

That's why systematically and intentionally setting aside a percentage of our income before we ever have a chance to *spend it is the most effective way to save money. In the same way the electric company took $400 before I ever had the chance to spend it, I want my savings and investment accounts to take money from me before I can spend it. I coach my clients to commit to saving 15-20% of their gross income and to automate the process to ensure that it happens consistently. Some clients wonder if they can survive off the remaining 80-85% of their income. Others are confident that they can. Regardless, nearly every client has success. Because we are so adaptable, we subconsciously modify our spending to meet the money that we have available, and typically never notice a difference in lifestyle. When I ask long-time clients where I've added the most value to their lives, I would assume they would point to their investments and the rates of return they've achieved. Instead, most point to cash flow prioritization and the fact that they're now able to successfully save significantly more money than ever before."*

Strategies for Effective Cash Flow Prioritization

1. **Protect Your Future:** First work to safeguard your assets and income from potential financial threats such as illness, injury, lawsuits, or premature death. This involves securing adequate Life and Disability

insurance, working to ensure sufficient liability coverage on home and auto policies, exploring umbrella policies, and setting up wills and trusts.

2. **Build a Life Events Fund:** Prioritize creating an accessible fund that covers six to twelve months of living expenses before addressing other financial goals. This fund serves as a financial cushion against unexpected events and helps preserve your savings.

3. **Focus on High-Impact Goals:** Prioritize financial objectives that have a significant impact on your long-term well-being. Contribute to retirement accounts, pay off high-interest debt, and save for major life goals before allocating funds to discretionary spending.

4. **Plan and Regularly Review Your Cash Flow:** Develop a comprehensive plan that outlines both income and expenses, including allocations for savings, debt repayment, and discretionary spending in the proper order. Regularly review and adjust this plan to stay on track with your financial goals.

5. **Avoid Lifestyle Creep:** When your income increases, resist the temptation to proportionally increase your spending. Instead, direct the additional income towards your savings goals. Committing to

save a percentage of your income (15-20%) rather than a fixed amount helps ensure that future income increases contribute to your savings.

Conclusion

Failing to prioritize our cash flow properly can seriously undermine our ability to save money and achieve financial stability. By understanding common pitfalls and implementing effective cash flow management strategies, we can ensure that our financial resources support both our immediate needs and long-term goals. Balancing and planning wisely helps us maintain a strong financial foundation.

Remember, the key to successful cash flow management is to plan wisely, prioritize effectively, and adjust as needed.

CONCLUSION

As we close out this journey together, it's evident that traditional saving methods—focused on hard work, sacrifice, and discipline—have failed millions of people. These approaches ignore the deeper personal values that drive our lasting decisions and behaviors. The result has historically been frustration and surrender.

We now know that most people struggle to save money because they haven't aligned their financial goals with the core values that are most important to them. Without this alignment, saving money becomes a chore rather than a meaningful pursuit. Coupled with the constant pressure to buy things in a consumer-driven world, saving money can feel nearly impossible. All the while, retailers exploit our buying urges, bombarding us with targeted ads across various platforms. To overcome this, we must shift our mindset and reframe how we think about and plan for our money.

One of the biggest keys comes in changing the way we prioritize our cash flow. If we continue to decide how much money to save after we decide how much money to spend, our ability to save money will always be limited. By setting aside a portion of money before addressing our lifestyle expenses, saving money becomes a priority rather than an afterthought. This shift can make saving money feel like less of a struggle and more systematic and intentional.

These conversations should be happening in the world of financial planning, but too often the discussions between advisors and clients begin and end with investing in the stock market. Knowing that the amount of money we can successfully save is more important to our future goals than the rate of return that we get from the stock market, more professionals in my industry should be helping their clients save more money before focusing on stocks and bonds. To put it plainly – Rate of Savings trumps Rate of Return. So why aren't more people investigating real-world solutions to keep more of the money they earn?

Thankfully, you're already one step ahead. By taking the time to read this book, you have already shown a commitment to getting a better grasp on your cash flow and are now equipped with cutting-edge strategies to break down the barriers that have stood in the way of you saving more money. Like other meaningful endeavors like career development, health and fitness and sports performance, the road to success is likely smoother with the assistance of a coach.

Let's keep the momentum going! By applying the insights from this book, you can realign your financial actions with your core values, making saving money both possible and rewarding. And for personalized advice tailored to your individual goals, reach out today. Call 813.289.3632 or email cgarrido@westshorefinancial.com. I'm here to help. Let's transform your financial dreams into reality. Your future self will thank you for the decisions you make today. The challenge of saving money doesn't have to define you financially.

.

ABOUT THE AUTHOR

Chris Garrido

Over the past decade, Chris Garrido has dedicated himself to serving his hometown of Tampa, FL, as a financial advisor, educator, and author. Many of the financial lessons he imparts were learned through the hard way, through personal experience, igniting a passion to teach others that financial wellness does not have to be difficult or complicated.

Chris is passionate about building healthy financial habits in the lives of his clients, allowing them to achieve financial balance and freedom. Opposed to the antiquated ways of his profession, Chris brings an uncommon, common-sense approach to money. Over the past decade, he has assisted hundreds of families and business owners in protecting, accumulating, and growing their wealth.

Though his time is limited as an advisor, author, husband, and father, Chris finds joy in coaching youth sports, supporting the University of Florida (his alma mater), fishing, and backyard BBQ. In retirement, he dreams of traveling across the country with his wife Felicia and competing in the barbecue competitions.

This material is intended for general public use. By providing this content, Park Avenue Securities LLC and your financial representative are not undertaking to provide investment advice or make a recommendation for a specific individual or situation, or to otherwise act in a fiduciary capacity. Guardian, its subsidiaries, agents, and employees do not provide tax, legal, or accounting advice. Consult your tax, legal, or accounting professional regarding your individual situation. Christian is a Registered Representative and Financial Advisor of Park Avenue Securities LLC (PAS). OSJ: 4200 W Cypress ST, Suite 700, Tampa FL, 33607, 813-289-3632. Securities products and advisory services offered through PAS, member FINRA, SIPC. Financial Representative of The Guardian Life Insurance Company of America® (Guardian), New York, NY. PAS is a wholly owned subsidiary of Guardian. Westshore Financial Group Inc is not an affiliate or subsidiary of PAS or Guardian. 6995665.1. This material has not been endorsed by Guardian, its subsidiaries, agents, or employees. No representation or warranty, either express or implied, is provided in relation to the accuracy, completeness, or reliability of the information contained herein. In addition, the content does not necessarily represent the opinions of Guardian, its subsidiaries, agents, or employees.

www.ingramcontent.com/pod-product-compliance
Lightning Source LLC
Chambersburg PA
CBHW070211230526
45471CB00002B/915